MW00875125

Driver Log Book

NAME:_____

EMAIL:_____

PHONE:_____

ADDRESS:_____

DRIVER LOG BOOK

DRIVERS NAME: _____ COMPANY: _____ WEEK: _____

TRUCK NUMBER	STARTING ODOMETER READING	ENDING ODOMETER READING	TOTAL DISTANCE

TRIP RECORD

DATE	TRAILER	ORIGIN CITY	DESTINATION CITY	MILES	RATE

TOTAL TRIPS: _____ TOTAL MILES: _____ TOTAL REVENUE: _____

FUEL PURCHASE RECORD

DATE	ODOMETER	MILES DRIVEN	GALLONS	MPG	RATE PER GALLON	TOTAL COST	NOTES

AVERAGE MILES PER GALLON: _____ AVERAGE COST OF FUEL PER GALLON: _____

MAINTENANCE RECORD

DATE	REPAIR FACILITY	REPAIRS DESCRIPTION	PO#	COST

NOTES:

DRIVER LOG BOOK

DRIVERS NAME: _____   COMPANY: _____   WEEK: _____

TRUCK NUMBER	STARTING ODOMETER READING	ENDING ODOMETER READING	TOTAL DISTANCE

TRIP RECORD

DATE	TRAILER	ORIGIN CITY	DESTINATION CITY	MILES	RATE

TOTAL TRIPS:_____   TOTAL MILES:_____   TOTAL REVENUE:_____

FUEL PURCHASE RECORD

DATE	ODOMETER	MILES DRIVEN	GALLONS	MPG	RATE PER GALLON	TOTAL COST	NOTES

AVERAGE MILES PER GALLON: _____   AVERAGE COST OF FUEL PER GALLON: _____

MAINTENANCE RECORD

DATE	REPAIR FACILITY	REPAIRS DESCRIPTION	PO#	COST

NOTES:

DRIVER LOG BOOK

DRIVERS NAME: _____   COMPANY: _____   WEEK: _____

TRUCK NUMBER	STARTING ODOMETER READING	ENDING ODOMETER READING	TOTAL DISTANCE

TRIP RECORD

DATE	TRAILER	ORIGIN CITY	DESTINATION CITY	MILES	RATE

TOTAL TRIPS: _____   TOTAL MILES: _____   TOTAL REVENUE: _____

FUEL PURCHASE RECORD

DATE	ODOMETER	MILES DRIVEN	GALLONS	MPG	RATE PER GALLON	TOTAL COST	NOTES

AVERAGE MILES PER GALLON: _____   AVERAGE COST OF FUEL PER GALLON: _____

MAINTENANCE RECORD

DATE	REPAIR FACILITY	REPAIRS DESCRIPTION	PO#	COST

NOTES:

DRIVER LOG BOOK

DRIVERS NAME: _____   COMPANY: _____   WEEK: _____

TRUCK NUMBER	STARTING ODOMETER READING	ENDING ODOMETER READING	TOTAL DISTANCE

TRIP RECORD

DATE	TRAILER	ORIGIN CITY	DESTINATION CITY	MILES	RATE

TOTAL TRIPS: _____   TOTAL MILES: _____   TOTAL REVENUE: _____

FUEL PURCHASE RECORD

DATE	ODOMETER	MILES DRIVEN	GALLONS	MPG	RATE PER GALLON	TOTAL COST	NOTES

AVERAGE MILES PER GALLON: _____   AVERAGE COST OF FUEL PER GALLON: _____

MAINTENANCE RECORD

DATE	REPAIR FACILITY	REPAIRS DESCRIPTION	PO#	COST

NOTES:

_____
_____
_____

Driver Log Book

DRIVERS NAME: _____   COMPANY: _____   WEEK: _____

TRUCK NUMBER	STARTING ODOMETER READING	ENDING ODOMETER READING	TOTAL DISTANCE

Trip Record

DATE	TRAILER	ORIGIN CITY	DESTINATION CITY	MILES	RATE

TOTAL TRIPS: _____   TOTAL MILES: _____   TOTAL REVENUE: _____

Fuel Purchase Record

DATE	ODOMETER	MILES DRIVEN	GALLONS	MPG	RATE PER GALLON	TOTAL COST	NOTES

AVERAGE MILES PER GALLON: _____   AVERAGE COST OF FUEL PER GALLON: _____

Maintenance Record

DATE	REPAIR FACILITY	REPAIRS DESCRIPTION	PO#	COST

NOTES:

Driver Log Book

DRIVERS NAME: _____   COMPANY: _____   WEEK: _____

TRUCK NUMBER	STARTING ODOMETER READING	ENDING ODOMETER READING	TOTAL DISTANCE

TRIP RECORD

DATE	TRAILER	ORIGIN CITY	DESTINATION CITY	MILES	RATE

TOTAL TRIPS: _____   TOTAL MILES: _____   TOTAL REVENUE: _____

FUEL PURCHASE RECORD

DATE	ODOMETER	MILES DRIVEN	GALLONS	MPG	RATE PER GALLON	TOTAL COST	NOTES

AVERAGE MILES PER GALLON: _____   AVERAGE COST OF FUEL PER GALLON: _____

MAINTENANCE RECORD

DATE	REPAIR FACILITY	REPAIRS DESCRIPTION	PO#	COST

NOTES:

_____

_____

_____

_____

Driver Log Book

Drivers Name: _____ Company: _____ Week: _____

Truck Number	Starting Odometer Reading	Ending Odometer Reading	Total Distance

Trip Record

Date	Trailer	Origin City	Destination City	Miles	Rate

Total Trips: _____ Total Miles: _____ Total Revenue: _____

Fuel Purchase Record

Date	Odometer	Miles Driven	Gallons	MPG	Rate Per Gallon	Total Cost	Notes

Average Miles Per Gallon: _____ Average Cost of Fuel Per Gallon: _____

Maintenance Record

Date	Repair Facility	Repairs Description	PO#	Cost

Notes:

Driver Log Book

DRIVERS NAME: _____ COMPANY: _____ WEEK: _____

TRUCK NUMBER	STARTING ODOMETER READING	ENDING ODOMETER READING	TOTAL DISTANCE

Trip Record

DATE	TRAILER	ORIGIN CITY	DESTINATION CITY	MILES	RATE

TOTAL TRIPS:_____ TOTAL MILES:_____ TOTAL REVENUE:_____

Fuel Purchase Record

DATE	ODOMETER	MILES DRIVEN	GALLONS	MPG	RATE PER GALLON	TOTAL COST	NOTES

AVERAGE MILES PER GALLON:_____ AVERAGE COST OF FUEL PER GALLON:_____

Maintenance Record

DATE	REPAIR FACILITY	REPAIRS DESCRIPTION	PO#	COST

NOTES:

_____

_____

_____

DRIVER LOG BOOK

DRIVERS NAME: _____   COMPANY: _____   WEEK: _____

TRUCK NUMBER	STARTING ODOMETER READING	ENDING ODOMETER READING	TOTAL DISTANCE

TRIP RECORD

DATE	TRAILER	ORIGIN CITY	DESTINATION CITY	MILES	RATE

TOTAL TRIPS: _____   TOTAL MILES: _____   TOTAL REVENUE: _____

FUEL PURCHASE RECORD

DATE	ODOMETER	MILES DRIVEN	GALLONS	MPG	RATE PER GALLON	TOTAL COST	NOTES

AVERAGE MILES PER GALLON: _____   AVERAGE COST OF FUEL PER GALLON: _____

MAINTENANCE RECORD

DATE	REPAIR FACILITY	REPAIRS DESCRIPTION	PO#	COST

NOTES:

DRIVER LOG BOOK

DRIVERS NAME: _____   COMPANY: _____   WEEK: _____

TRUCK NUMBER	STARTING ODOMETER READING	ENDING ODOMETER READING	TOTAL DISTANCE

TRIP RECORD

DATE	TRAILER	ORIGIN CITY	DESTINATION CITY	MILES	RATE

TOTAL TRIPS:_____   TOTAL MILES:_____   TOTAL REVENUE:_____

FUEL PURCHASE RECORD

DATE	ODOMETER	MILES DRIVEN	GALLONS	MPG	RATE PER GALLON	TOTAL COST	NOTES

AVERAGE MILES PER GALLON: _____   AVERAGE COST OF FUEL PER GALLON: _____

MAINTENANCE RECORD

DATE	REPAIR FACILITY	REPAIRS DESCRIPTION	PO#	COST

NOTES:

_____

_____

_____

Driver Log Book

DRIVERS NAME: _____ COMPANY: _____ WEEK: _____

TRUCK NUMBER	STARTING ODOMETER READING	ENDING ODOMETER READING	TOTAL DISTANCE

Trip Record

DATE	TRAILER	ORIGIN CITY	DESTINATION CITY	MILES	RATE

TOTAL TRIPS: _____ TOTAL MILES: _____ TOTAL REVENUE: _____

Fuel Purchase Record

DATE	ODOMETER	MILES DRIVEN	GALLONS	MPG	RATE PER GALLON	TOTAL COST	NOTES

AVERAGE MILES PER GALLON: _____ AVERAGE COST OF FUEL PER GALLON: _____

Maintenance Record

DATE	REPAIR FACILITY	REPAIRS DESCRIPTION	PO#	COST

NOTES:

Driver Log Book

DRIVERS NAME: _____   COMPANY: _____   WEEK: _____

TRUCK NUMBER	STARTING ODOMETER READING	ENDING ODOMETER READING	TOTAL DISTANCE

TRIP RECORD

DATE	TRAILER	ORIGIN CITY	DESTINATION CITY	MILES	RATE

TOTAL TRIPS: _____   TOTAL MILES: _____   TOTAL REVENUE: _____

FUEL PURCHASE RECORD

DATE	ODOMETER	MILES DRIVEN	GALLONS	MPG	RATE PER GALLON	TOTAL COST	NOTES

AVERAGE MILES PER GALLON: _____   AVERAGE COST OF FUEL PER GALLON: _____

MAINTENANCE RECORD

DATE	REPAIR FACILITY	REPAIRS DESCRIPTION	PO#	COST

NOTES:

_____

_____

_____

Driver Log Book

DRIVERS NAME: _____   COMPANY: _____   WEEK: _____

TRUCK NUMBER	STARTING ODOMETER READING	ENDING ODOMETER READING	TOTAL DISTANCE

Trip Record

DATE	TRAILER	ORIGIN CITY	DESTINATION CITY	MILES	RATE

TOTAL TRIPS: _____   TOTAL MILES: _____   TOTAL REVENUE: _____

Fuel Purchase Record

DATE	ODOMETER	MILES DRIVEN	GALLONS	MPG	RATE PER GALLON	TOTAL COST	NOTES

AVERAGE MILES PER GALLON: _____   AVERAGE COST OF FUEL PER GALLON: _____

Maintenance Record

DATE	REPAIR FACILITY	REPAIRS DESCRIPTION	PO#	COST

NOTES:

DRIVER LOG BOOK

DRIVERS NAME: _____   COMPANY: _____   WEEK: _____

TRUCK NUMBER	STARTING ODOMETER READING	ENDING ODOMETER READING	TOTAL DISTANCE

TRIP RECORD

DATE	TRAILER	ORIGIN CITY	DESTINATION CITY	MILES	RATE

TOTAL TRIPS: _____   TOTAL MILES: _____   TOTAL REVENUE: _____

FUEL PURCHASE RECORD

DATE	ODOMETER	MILES DRIVEN	GALLONS	MPG	RATE PER GALLON	TOTAL COST	NOTES

AVERAGE MILES PER GALLON: _____   AVERAGE COST OF FUEL PER GALLON: _____

MAINTENANCE RECORD

DATE	REPAIR FACILITY	REPAIRS DESCRIPTION	PO#	COST

NOTES: _____
_____
_____
_____
_____

Driver Log Book

DRIVERS NAME: _____ COMPANY: _____ WEEK: _____

TRUCK NUMBER	STARTING ODOMETER READING	ENDING ODOMETER READING	TOTAL DISTANCE

Trip Record

DATE	TRAILER	ORIGIN CITY	DESTINATION CITY	MILES	RATE

TOTAL TRIPS: _____ TOTAL MILES: _____ TOTAL REVENUE: _____

Fuel Purchase Record

DATE	ODOMETER	MILES DRIVEN	GALLONS	MPG	RATE PER GALLON	TOTAL COST	NOTES

AVERAGE MILES PER GALLON: _____ AVERAGE COST OF FUEL PER GALLON: _____

Maintenance Record

DATE	REPAIR FACILITY	REPAIRS DESCRIPTION	PO#	COST

NOTES:

Driver Log Book

Drivers Name: _____   Company: _____   Week: _____

Truck Number	Starting Odometer Reading	Ending Odometer Reading	Total Distance

Trip Record

Date	Trailer	Origin City	Destination City	Miles	Rate

Total Trips: _____   Total Miles: _____   Total Revenue: _____

Fuel Purchase Record

Date	Odometer	Miles Driven	Gallons	MPG	Rate Per Gallon	Total Cost	Notes

Average Miles Per Gallon: _____   Average Cost of Fuel Per Gallon: _____

Maintenance Record

Date	Repair Facility	Repairs Description	PO#	Cost

Notes:

_____

_____

_____

_____

DRIVER LOG BOOK

DRIVERS NAME: _____ COMPANY: _____ WEEK: _____

TRUCK NUMBER	STARTING ODOMETER READING	ENDING ODOMETER READING	TOTAL DISTANCE

TRIP RECORD

DATE	TRAILER	ORIGIN CITY	DESTINATION CITY	MILES	RATE

TOTAL TRIPS: _____ TOTAL MILES: _____ TOTAL REVENUE: _____

FUEL PURCHASE RECORD

DATE	ODOMETER	MILES DRIVEN	GALLONS	MPG	RATE PER GALLON	TOTAL COST	NOTES

AVERAGE MILES PER GALLON: _____ AVERAGE COST OF FUEL PER GALLON: _____

MAINTENANCE RECORD

DATE	REPAIR FACILITY	REPAIRS DESCRIPTION	PO#	COST

NOTES:

DRIVER LOG BOOK

DRIVERS NAME: _____   COMPANY: _____   WEEK: _____

TRUCK NUMBER	STARTING ODOMETER READING	ENDING ODOMETER READING	TOTAL DISTANCE

TRIP RECORD

DATE	TRAILER	ORIGIN CITY	DESTINATION CITY	MILES	RATE

TOTAL TRIPS: _____   TOTAL MILES: _____   TOTAL REVENUE: _____

FUEL PURCHASE RECORD

DATE	ODOMETER	MILES DRIVEN	GALLONS	MPG	RATE PER GALLON	TOTAL COST	NOTES

AVERAGE MILES PER GALLON: _____   AVERAGE COST OF FUEL PER GALLON: _____

MAINTENANCE RECORD

DATE	REPAIR FACILITY	REPAIRS DESCRIPTION	PO#	COST

NOTES:

_____

_____

_____

DRIVER LOG BOOK

DRIVERS NAME: _____   COMPANY: _____   WEEK: _____

TRUCK NUMBER	STARTING ODOMETER READING	ENDING ODOMETER READING	TOTAL DISTANCE

TRIP RECORD

DATE	TRAILER	ORIGIN CITY	DESTINATION CITY	MILES	RATE

TOTAL TRIPS: _____   TOTAL MILES: _____   TOTAL REVENUE: _____

FUEL PURCHASE RECORD

DATE	ODOMETER	MILES DRIVEN	GALLONS	MPG	RATE PER GALLON	TOTAL COST	NOTES

AVERAGE MILES PER GALLON: _____   AVERAGE COST OF FUEL PER GALLON: _____

MAINTENANCE RECORD

DATE	REPAIR FACILITY	REPAIRS DESCRIPTION	PO#	COST

NOTES:

DRIVER LOG BOOK

DRIVERS NAME: _____   COMPANY: _____   WEEK: _____

TRUCK NUMBER	STARTING ODOMETER READING	ENDING ODOMETER READING	TOTAL DISTANCE

TRIP RECORD

DATE	TRAILER	ORIGIN CITY	DESTINATION CITY	MILES	RATE

TOTAL TRIPS: _____   TOTAL MILES: _____   TOTAL REVENUE: _____

FUEL PURCHASE RECORD

DATE	ODOMETER	MILES DRIVEN	GALLONS	MPG	RATE PER GALLON	TOTAL COST	NOTES

AVERAGE MILES PER GALLON: _____   AVERAGE COST OF FUEL PER GALLON: _____

MAINTENANCE RECORD

DATE	REPAIR FACILITY	REPAIRS DESCRIPTION	PO#	COST

NOTES:

_____
_____
_____

DRIVER LOG BOOK

DRIVERS NAME: _____   COMPANY: _____   WEEK: _____

TRUCK NUMBER	STARTING ODOMETER READING	ENDING ODOMETER READING	TOTAL DISTANCE

TRIP RECORD

DATE	TRAILER	ORIGIN CITY	DESTINATION CITY	MILES	RATE

TOTAL TRIPS: _____   TOTAL MILES: _____   TOTAL REVENUE: _____

FUEL PURCHASE RECORD

DATE	ODOMETER	MILES DRIVEN	GALLONS	MPG	RATE PER GALLON	TOTAL COST	NOTES

AVERAGE MILES PER GALLON: _____   AVERAGE COST OF FUEL PER GALLON: _____

MAINTENANCE RECORD

DATE	REPAIR FACILITY	REPAIRS DESCRIPTION	PO#	COST

NOTES:

Driver Log Book

DRIVERS NAME: _____   COMPANY: _____   WEEK: _____

TRUCK NUMBER	STARTING ODOMETER READING	ENDING ODOMETER READING	TOTAL DISTANCE

TRIP RECORD

DATE	TRAILER	ORIGIN CITY	DESTINATION CITY	MILES	RATE

TOTAL TRIPS: _____   TOTAL MILES: _____   TOTAL REVENUE: _____

FUEL PURCHASE RECORD

DATE	ODOMETER	MILES DRIVEN	GALLONS	MPG	RATE PER GALLON	TOTAL COST	NOTES

AVERAGE MILES PER GALLON: _____   AVERAGE COST OF FUEL PER GALLON: _____

MAINTENANCE RECORD

DATE	REPAIR FACILITY	REPAIRS DESCRIPTION	PO#	COST

NOTES:

_____

_____

_____

Driver Log Book

DRIVERS NAME: _____ COMPANY: _____ WEEK: _____

TRUCK NUMBER	STARTING ODOMETER READING	ENDING ODOMETER READING	TOTAL DISTANCE

Trip Record

Date	Trailer	Origin City	Destination City	Miles	Rate

TOTAL TRIPS: _____ TOTAL MILES: _____ TOTAL REVENUE: _____

Fuel Purchase Record

Date	Odometer	Miles Driven	Gallons	MPG	Rate Per Gallon	Total Cost	Notes

AVERAGE MILES PER GALLON: _____ AVERAGE COST OF FUEL PER GALLON: _____

Maintenance Record

Date	Repair Facility	Repairs Description	PO#	Cost

NOTES: _____

_____

_____

_____

Driver Log Book

DRIVERS NAME: _____ COMPANY: _____ WEEK: _____

TRUCK NUMBER	STARTING ODOMETER READING	ENDING ODOMETER READING	TOTAL DISTANCE

Trip Record

DATE	TRAILER	ORIGIN CITY	DESTINATION CITY	MILES	RATE

TOTAL TRIPS:_____ TOTAL MILES:_____ TOTAL REVENUE:_____

Fuel Purchase Record

DATE	ODOMETER	MILES DRIVEN	GALLONS	MPG	RATE PER GALLON	TOTAL COST	NOTES

AVERAGE MILES PER GALLON: _____ AVERAGE COST OF FUEL PER GALLON: _____

Maintenance Record

DATE	REPAIR FACILITY	REPAIRS DESCRIPTION	PO#	COST

NOTES:

_____

_____

_____

Driver Log Book

DRIVERS NAME: _____   COMPANY: _____   WEEK: _____

TRUCK NUMBER	STARTING ODOMETER READING	ENDING ODOMETER READING	TOTAL DISTANCE

Trip Record

DATE	TRAILER	ORIGIN CITY	DESTINATION CITY	MILES	RATE

TOTAL TRIPS: _____   TOTAL MILES: _____   TOTAL REVENUE: _____

Fuel Purchase Record

DATE	ODOMETER	MILES DRIVEN	GALLONS	MPG	RATE PER GALLON	TOTAL COST	NOTES

AVERAGE MILES PER GALLON: _____   AVERAGE COST OF FUEL PER GALLON: _____

Maintenance Record

DATE	REPAIR FACILITY	REPAIRS DESCRIPTION	PO#	COST

NOTES:

Driver Log Book

DRIVERS NAME: _____   COMPANY: _____   WEEK: _____

TRUCK NUMBER	STARTING ODOMETER READING	ENDING ODOMETER READING	TOTAL DISTANCE

TRIP RECORD

DATE	TRAILER	ORIGIN CITY	DESTINATION CITY	MILES	RATE

TOTAL TRIPS: _____   TOTAL MILES: _____   TOTAL REVENUE: _____

FUEL PURCHASE RECORD

DATE	ODOMETER	MILES DRIVEN	GALLONS	MPG	RATE PER GALLON	TOTAL COST	NOTES

AVERAGE MILES PER GALLON: _____   AVERAGE COST OF FUEL PER GALLON: _____

MAINTENANCE RECORD

DATE	REPAIR FACILITY	REPAIRS DESCRIPTION	PO#	COST

NOTES:

_____

_____

_____

DRIVER LOG BOOK

DRIVERS NAME: _____   COMPANY: _____   WEEK: _____

TRUCK NUMBER	STARTING ODOMETER READING	ENDING ODOMETER READING	TOTAL DISTANCE

TRIP RECORD

DATE	TRAILER	ORIGIN CITY	DESTINATION CITY	MILES	RATE

TOTAL TRIPS: _____   TOTAL MILES: _____   TOTAL REVENUE: _____

FUEL PURCHASE RECORD

DATE	ODOMETER	MILES DRIVEN	GALLONS	MPG	RATE PER GALLON	TOTAL COST	NOTES

AVERAGE MILES PER GALLON: _____   AVERAGE COST OF FUEL PER GALLON: _____

MAINTENANCE RECORD

DATE	REPAIR FACILITY	REPAIRS DESCRIPTION	PO#	COST

NOTES:

Driver Log Book

DRIVERS NAME: _____   COMPANY: _____   WEEK: _____

TRUCK NUMBER	STARTING ODOMETER READING	ENDING ODOMETER READING	TOTAL DISTANCE

TRIP RECORD

DATE	TRAILER	ORIGIN CITY	DESTINATION CITY	MILES	RATE

TOTAL TRIPS:_____   TOTAL MILES:_____   TOTAL REVENUE:_____

FUEL PURCHASE RECORD

DATE	ODOMETER	MILES DRIVEN	GALLONS	MPG	RATE PER GALLON	TOTAL COST	NOTES

AVERAGE MILES PER GALLON: _____   AVERAGE COST OF FUEL PER GALLON: _____

MAINTENANCE RECORD

DATE	REPAIR FACILITY	REPAIRS DESCRIPTION	PO#	COST

NOTES:

_____

_____

_____

DRIVER LOG BOOK

DRIVERS NAME: _____ COMPANY: _____ WEEK: _____

TRUCK NUMBER	STARTING ODOMETER READING	ENDING ODOMETER READING	TOTAL DISTANCE

TRIP RECORD

DATE	TRAILER	ORIGIN CITY	DESTINATION CITY	MILES	RATE

TOTAL TRIPS: _____ TOTAL MILES: _____ TOTAL REVENUE: _____

FUEL PURCHASE RECORD

DATE	ODOMETER	MILES DRIVEN	GALLONS	MPG	RATE PER GALLON	TOTAL COST	NOTES

AVERAGE MILES PER GALLON: _____ AVERAGE COST OF FUEL PER GALLON: _____

MAINTENANCE RECORD

DATE	REPAIR FACILITY	REPAIRS DESCRIPTION	PO#	COST

NOTES:

Driver Log Book

DRIVERS NAME: _____ COMPANY: _____ WEEK: _____

TRUCK NUMBER	STARTING ODOMETER READING	ENDING ODOMETER READING	TOTAL DISTANCE

TRIP RECORD

DATE	TRAILER	ORIGIN CITY	DESTINATION CITY	MILES	RATE

TOTAL TRIPS:_____ TOTAL MILES:_____ TOTAL REVENUE:_____

FUEL PURCHASE RECORD

DATE	ODOMETER	MILES DRIVEN	GALLONS	MPG	RATE PER GALLON	TOTAL COST	NOTES

AVERAGE MILES PER GALLON: _____ AVERAGE COST OF FUEL PER GALLON: _____

MAINTENANCE RECORD

DATE	REPAIR FACILITY	REPAIRS DESCRIPTION	PO#	COST

NOTES:

_____

_____

_____

DRIVER LOG BOOK

DRIVERS NAME: _____   COMPANY: _____   WEEK: _____

TRUCK NUMBER	STARTING ODOMETER READING	ENDING ODOMETER READING	TOTAL DISTANCE

TRIP RECORD

DATE	TRAILER	ORIGIN CITY	DESTINATION CITY	MILES	RATE

TOTAL TRIPS: _____   TOTAL MILES: _____   TOTAL REVENUE: _____

FUEL PURCHASE RECORD

DATE	ODOMETER	MILES DRIVEN	GALLONS	MPG	RATE PER GALLON	TOTAL COST	NOTES

AVERAGE MILES PER GALLON: _____   AVERAGE COST OF FUEL PER GALLON: _____

MAINTENANCE RECORD

DATE	REPAIR FACILITY	REPAIRS DESCRIPTION	PO#	COST

NOTES:

Driver Log Book

DRIVERS NAME: _____ COMPANY: _____ WEEK: _____

TRUCK NUMBER	STARTING ODOMETER READING	ENDING ODOMETER READING	TOTAL DISTANCE

TRIP RECORD

DATE	TRAILER	ORIGIN CITY	DESTINATION CITY	MILES	RATE

TOTAL TRIPS:_____ TOTAL MILES:_____ TOTAL REVENUE:_____

FUEL PURCHASE RECORD

DATE	ODOMETER	MILES DRIVEN	GALLONS	MPG	RATE PER GALLON	TOTAL COST	NOTES

AVERAGE MILES PER GALLON: _____ AVERAGE COST OF FUEL PER GALLON: _____

MAINTENANCE RECORD

DATE	REPAIR FACILITY	REPAIRS DESCRIPTION	PO#	COST

NOTES:
_____
_____
_____

DRIVER LOG BOOK

DRIVERS NAME: _____ COMPANY: _____ WEEK: _____

TRUCK NUMBER	STARTING ODOMETER READING	ENDING ODOMETER READING	TOTAL DISTANCE

TRIP RECORD

DATE	TRAILER	ORIGIN CITY	DESTINATION CITY	MILES	RATE

TOTAL TRIPS: _____ TOTAL MILES: _____ TOTAL REVENUE: _____

FUEL PURCHASE RECORD

DATE	ODOMETER	MILES DRIVEN	GALLONS	MPG	RATE PER GALLON	TOTAL COST	NOTES

AVERAGE MILES PER GALLON: _____ AVERAGE COST OF FUEL PER GALLON: _____

MAINTENANCE RECORD

DATE	REPAIR FACILITY	REPAIRS DESCRIPTION	PO#	COST

NOTES:

Driver Log Book

DRIVERS NAME: _____   COMPANY: _____   WEEK: _____

TRUCK NUMBER	STARTING ODOMETER READING	ENDING ODOMETER READING	TOTAL DISTANCE

TRIP RECORD

DATE	TRAILER	ORIGIN CITY	DESTINATION CITY	MILES	RATE

TOTAL TRIPS: _____   TOTAL MILES: _____   TOTAL REVENUE: _____

FUEL PURCHASE RECORD

DATE	ODOMETER	MILES DRIVEN	GALLONS	MPG	RATE PER GALLON	TOTAL COST	NOTES

AVERAGE MILES PER GALLON: _____   AVERAGE COST OF FUEL PER GALLON: _____

MAINTENANCE RECORD

DATE	REPAIR FACILITY	REPAIRS DESCRIPTION	PO#	COST

NOTES:

_____

_____

_____

_____

DRIVER LOG BOOK

DRIVERS NAME: _____   COMPANY: _____   WEEK: _____

TRUCK NUMBER	STARTING ODOMETER READING	ENDING ODOMETER READING	TOTAL DISTANCE

TRIP RECORD

DATE	TRAILER	ORIGIN CITY	DESTINATION CITY	MILES	RATE

TOTAL TRIPS: _____   TOTAL MILES: _____   TOTAL REVENUE: _____

FUEL PURCHASE RECORD

DATE	ODOMETER	MILES DRIVEN	GALLONS	MPG	RATE PER GALLON	TOTAL COST	NOTES

AVERAGE MILES PER GALLON: _____   AVERAGE COST OF FUEL PER GALLON: _____

MAINTENANCE RECORD

DATE	REPAIR FACILITY	REPAIRS DESCRIPTION	PO#	COST

NOTES:

DRIVER LOG BOOK

DRIVERS NAME: _____   COMPANY: _____   WEEK: _____

TRUCK NUMBER	STARTING ODOMETER READING	ENDING ODOMETER READING	TOTAL DISTANCE

TRIP RECORD

DATE	TRAILER	ORIGIN CITY	DESTINATION CITY	MILES	RATE

TOTAL TRIPS: _____   TOTAL MILES: _____   TOTAL REVENUE: _____

FUEL PURCHASE RECORD

DATE	ODOMETER	MILES DRIVEN	GALLONS	MPG	RATE PER GALLON	TOTAL COST	NOTES

AVERAGE MILES PER GALLON: _____   AVERAGE COST OF FUEL PER GALLON: _____

MAINTENANCE RECORD

DATE	REPAIR FACILITY	REPAIRS DESCRIPTION	PO#	COST

NOTES:

_____

_____

_____

_____

DRIVER LOG BOOK

DRIVERS NAME: _____ COMPANY: _____ WEEK: _____

TRUCK NUMBER	STARTING ODOMETER READING	ENDING ODOMETER READING	TOTAL DISTANCE

TRIP RECORD

DATE	TRAILER	ORIGIN CITY	DESTINATION CITY	MILES	RATE

TOTAL TRIPS:_____ TOTAL MILES:_____ TOTAL REVENUE:_____

FUEL PURCHASE RECORD

DATE	ODOMETER	MILES DRIVEN	GALLONS	MPG	RATE PER GALLON	TOTAL COST	NOTES

AVERAGE MILES PER GALLON: _____ AVERAGE COST OF FUEL PER GALLON: _____

MAINTENANCE RECORD

DATE	REPAIR FACILITY	REPAIRS DESCRIPTION	PO#	COST

NOTES:

DRIVER LOG BOOK

DRIVERS NAME: _____   COMPANY: _____   WEEK: _____

TRUCK NUMBER	STARTING ODOMETER READING	ENDING ODOMETER READING	TOTAL DISTANCE

TRIP RECORD

DATE	TRAILER	ORIGIN CITY	DESTINATION CITY	MILES	RATE

TOTAL TRIPS: _____   TOTAL MILES: _____   TOTAL REVENUE: _____

FUEL PURCHASE RECORD

DATE	ODOMETER	MILES DRIVEN	GALLONS	MPG	RATE PER GALLON	TOTAL COST	NOTES

AVERAGE MILES PER GALLON: _____   AVERAGE COST OF FUEL PER GALLON: _____

MAINTENANCE RECORD

DATE	REPAIR FACILITY	REPAIRS DESCRIPTION	PO#	COST

NOTES:

_____

_____

_____

_____

Driver Log Book

DRIVERS NAME: _____   COMPANY: _____   WEEK: _____

TRUCK NUMBER	STARTING ODOMETER READING	ENDING ODOMETER READING	TOTAL DISTANCE

TRIP RECORD

DATE	TRAILER	ORIGIN CITY	DESTINATION CITY	MILES	RATE

TOTAL TRIPS: _____   TOTAL MILES: _____   TOTAL REVENUE: _____

FUEL PURCHASE RECORD

DATE	ODOMETER	MILES DRIVEN	GALLONS	MPG	RATE PER GALLON	TOTAL COST	NOTES

AVERAGE MILES PER GALLON: _____   AVERAGE COST OF FUEL PER GALLON: _____

MAINTENANCE RECORD

DATE	REPAIR FACILITY	REPAIRS DESCRIPTION	PO#	COST

NOTES:

Driver Log Book

DRIVERS NAME: _____   COMPANY: _____   WEEK: _____

TRUCK NUMBER	STARTING ODOMETER READING	ENDING ODOMETER READING	TOTAL DISTANCE

TRIP RECORD

DATE	TRAILER	ORIGIN CITY	DESTINATION CITY	MILES	RATE

TOTAL TRIPS: _____   TOTAL MILES: _____   TOTAL REVENUE: _____

FUEL PURCHASE RECORD

DATE	ODOMETER	MILES DRIVEN	GALLONS	MPG	RATE PER GALLON	TOTAL COST	NOTES

AVERAGE MILES PER GALLON: _____   AVERAGE COST OF FUEL PER GALLON: _____

MAINTENANCE RECORD

DATE	REPAIR FACILITY	REPAIRS DESCRIPTION	PO#	COST

NOTES:

Driver Log Book

DRIVERS NAME: _____   COMPANY: _____   WEEK: _____

TRUCK NUMBER	STARTING ODOMETER READING	ENDING ODOMETER READING	TOTAL DISTANCE

Trip Record

DATE	TRAILER	ORIGIN CITY	DESTINATION CITY	MILES	RATE

TOTAL TRIPS: _____   TOTAL MILES: _____   TOTAL REVENUE: _____

Fuel Purchase Record

DATE	ODOMETER	MILES DRIVEN	GALLONS	MPG	RATE PER GALLON	TOTAL COST	NOTES

AVERAGE MILES PER GALLON: _____   AVERAGE COST OF FUEL PER GALLON: _____

Maintenance Record

DATE	REPAIR FACILITY	REPAIRS DESCRIPTION	PO#	COST

NOTES:

Driver Log Book

DRIVERS NAME: _____ COMPANY: _____ WEEK: _____

TRUCK NUMBER	STARTING ODOMETER READING	ENDING ODOMETER READING	TOTAL DISTANCE

Trip Record

DATE	TRAILER	ORIGIN CITY	DESTINATION CITY	MILES	RATE

TOTAL TRIPS: _____ TOTAL MILES: _____ TOTAL REVENUE: _____

Fuel Purchase Record

DATE	ODOMETER	MILES DRIVEN	GALLONS	MPG	RATE PER GALLON	TOTAL COST	NOTES

AVERAGE MILES PER GALLON: _____ AVERAGE COST OF FUEL PER GALLON: _____

Maintenance Record

DATE	REPAIR FACILITY	REPAIRS DESCRIPTION	PO#	COST

NOTES:

_____

_____

_____

DRIVER LOG BOOK

DRIVERS NAME: _____   COMPANY: _____   WEEK: _____

TRUCK NUMBER	STARTING ODOMETER READING	ENDING ODOMETER READING	TOTAL DISTANCE

TRIP RECORD

DATE	TRAILER	ORIGIN CITY	DESTINATION CITY	MILES	RATE

TOTAL TRIPS: _____   TOTAL MILES: _____   TOTAL REVENUE: _____

FUEL PURCHASE RECORD

DATE	ODOMETER	MILES DRIVEN	GALLONS	MPG	RATE PER GALLON	TOTAL COST	NOTES

AVERAGE MILES PER GALLON: _____   AVERAGE COST OF FUEL PER GALLON: _____

MAINTENANCE RECORD

DATE	REPAIR FACILITY	REPAIRS DESCRIPTION	PO#	COST

NOTES:

Driver Log Book

DRIVERS NAME: _____   COMPANY: _____   WEEK: _____

TRUCK NUMBER	STARTING ODOMETER READING	ENDING ODOMETER READING	TOTAL DISTANCE

TRIP RECORD

DATE	TRAILER	ORIGIN CITY	DESTINATION CITY	MILES	RATE

TOTAL TRIPS:_____   TOTAL MILES:_____   TOTAL REVENUE:_____

FUEL PURCHASE RECORD

DATE	ODOMETER	MILES DRIVEN	GALLONS	MPG	RATE PER GALLON	TOTAL COST	NOTES

AVERAGE MILES PER GALLON: _____   AVERAGE COST OF FUEL PER GALLON: _____

MAINTENANCE RECORD

DATE	REPAIR FACILITY	REPAIRS DESCRIPTION	PO#	COST

NOTES:

_____

_____

_____

Driver Log Book

DRIVERS NAME: _____   COMPANY: _____   WEEK: _____

TRUCK NUMBER	STARTING ODOMETER READING	ENDING ODOMETER READING	TOTAL DISTANCE

TRIP RECORD

DATE	TRAILER	ORIGIN CITY	DESTINATION CITY	MILES	RATE

TOTAL TRIPS: _____   TOTAL MILES: _____   TOTAL REVENUE: _____

FUEL PURCHASE RECORD

DATE	ODOMETER	MILES DRIVEN	GALLONS	MPG	RATE PER GALLON	TOTAL COST	NOTES

AVERAGE MILES PER GALLON: _____   AVERAGE COST OF FUEL PER GALLON: _____

MAINTENANCE RECORD

DATE	REPAIR FACILITY	REPAIRS DESCRIPTION	PO#	COST

NOTES:

Driver Log Book

DRIVERS NAME: _____ COMPANY: _____ WEEK: _____

Truck Number	Starting Odometer Reading	Ending Odometer Reading	Total Distance

Trip Record

Date	Trailer	Origin City	Destination City	Miles	Rate

TOTAL TRIPS: _____ TOTAL MILES: _____ TOTAL REVENUE: _____

Fuel Purchase Record

Date	Odometer	Miles Driven	Gallons	MPG	Rate Per Gallon	Total Cost	Notes

AVERAGE MILES PER GALLON: _____ AVERAGE COST OF FUEL PER GALLON: _____

Maintenance Record

Date	Repair Facility	Repairs Description	PO#	Cost

NOTES: _____

_____

_____

_____

DRIVER LOG BOOK

DRIVERS NAME: _____   COMPANY: _____   WEEK: _____

TRUCK NUMBER	STARTING ODOMETER READING	ENDING ODOMETER READING	TOTAL DISTANCE

TRIP RECORD

DATE	TRAILER	ORIGIN CITY	DESTINATION CITY	MILES	RATE

TOTAL TRIPS: _____   TOTAL MILES: _____   TOTAL REVENUE: _____

FUEL PURCHASE RECORD

DATE	ODOMETER	MILES DRIVEN	GALLONS	MPG	RATE PER GALLON	TOTAL COST	NOTES

AVERAGE MILES PER GALLON: _____   AVERAGE COST OF FUEL PER GALLON: _____

MAINTENANCE RECORD

DATE	REPAIR FACILITY	REPAIRS DESCRIPTION	PO#	COST

NOTES:

DRIVER LOG BOOK

DRIVERS NAME: _____   COMPANY: _____   WEEK: _____

TRUCK NUMBER	STARTING ODOMETER READING	ENDING ODOMETER READING	TOTAL DISTANCE

TRIP RECORD

DATE	TRAILER	ORIGIN CITY	DESTINATION CITY	MILES	RATE

TOTAL TRIPS:_____   TOTAL MILES:_____   TOTAL REVENUE:_____

FUEL PURCHASE RECORD

DATE	ODOMETER	MILES DRIVEN	GALLONS	MPG	RATE PER GALLON	TOTAL COST	NOTES

AVERAGE MILES PER GALLON: _____   AVERAGE COST OF FUEL PER GALLON: _____

MAINTENANCE RECORD

DATE	REPAIR FACILITY	REPAIRS DESCRIPTION	PO#	COST

NOTES:

_____

_____

_____

Driver Log Book

DRIVERS NAME: _____ COMPANY: _____ WEEK: _____

TRUCK NUMBER	STARTING ODOMETER READING	ENDING ODOMETER READING	TOTAL DISTANCE

Trip Record

DATE	TRAILER	ORIGIN CITY	DESTINATION CITY	MILES	RATE

TOTAL TRIPS: _____ TOTAL MILES: _____ TOTAL REVENUE: _____

Fuel Purchase Record

DATE	ODOMETER	MILES DRIVEN	GALLONS	MPG	RATE PER GALLON	TOTAL COST	NOTES

AVERAGE MILES PER GALLON: _____ AVERAGE COST OF FUEL PER GALLON: _____

Maintenance Record

DATE	REPAIR FACILITY	REPAIRS DESCRIPTION	PO#	COST

NOTES:

Driver Log Book

DRIVERS NAME: _____   COMPANY: _____   WEEK: _____

TRUCK NUMBER	STARTING ODOMETER READING	ENDING ODOMETER READING	TOTAL DISTANCE

TRIP RECORD

DATE	TRAILER	ORIGIN CITY	DESTINATION CITY	MILES	RATE

TOTAL TRIPS: _____   TOTAL MILES: _____   TOTAL REVENUE: _____

FUEL PURCHASE RECORD

DATE	ODOMETER	MILES DRIVEN	GALLONS	MPG	RATE PER GALLON	TOTAL COST	NOTES

AVERAGE MILES PER GALLON: _____   AVERAGE COST OF FUEL PER GALLON: _____

MAINTENANCE RECORD

DATE	REPAIR FACILITY	REPAIRS DESCRIPTION	PO#	COST

NOTES:

_____

_____

_____

_____

DRIVER LOG BOOK

DRIVERS NAME: _____   COMPANY: _____   WEEK: _____

TRUCK NUMBER	STARTING ODOMETER READING	ENDING ODOMETER READING	TOTAL DISTANCE

TRIP RECORD

DATE	TRAILER	ORIGIN CITY	DESTINATION CITY	MILES	RATE

TOTAL TRIPS: _____   TOTAL MILES: _____   TOTAL REVENUE: _____

FUEL PURCHASE RECORD

DATE	ODOMETER	MILES DRIVEN	GALLONS	MPG	RATE PER GALLON	TOTAL COST	NOTES

AVERAGE MILES PER GALLON: _____   AVERAGE COST OF FUEL PER GALLON: _____

MAINTENANCE RECORD

DATE	REPAIR FACILITY	REPAIRS DESCRIPTION	PO#	COST

NOTES:

Driver Log Book

DRIVERS NAME: _____ COMPANY: _____ WEEK: _____

TRUCK NUMBER	STARTING ODOMETER READING	ENDING ODOMETER READING	TOTAL DISTANCE

Trip Record

DATE	TRAILER	ORIGIN CITY	DESTINATION CITY	MILES	RATE

TOTAL TRIPS: _____ TOTAL MILES: _____ TOTAL REVENUE: _____

Fuel Purchase Record

DATE	ODOMETER	MILES DRIVEN	GALLONS	MPG	RATE PER GALLON	TOTAL COST	NOTES

AVERAGE MILES PER GALLON: _____ AVERAGE COST OF FUEL PER GALLON: _____

Maintenance Record

DATE	REPAIR FACILITY	REPAIRS DESCRIPTION	PO#	COST

NOTES:

_____

_____

_____

DRIVER LOG BOOK

DRIVERS NAME: _____ COMPANY: _____ WEEK: _____

TRUCK NUMBER	STARTING ODOMETER READING	ENDING ODOMETER READING	TOTAL DISTANCE

TRIP RECORD

DATE	TRAILER	ORIGIN CITY	DESTINATION CITY	MILES	RATE

TOTAL TRIPS: _____ TOTAL MILES: _____ TOTAL REVENUE: _____

FUEL PURCHASE RECORD

DATE	ODOMETER	MILES DRIVEN	GALLONS	MPG	RATE PER GALLON	TOTAL COST	NOTES

AVERAGE MILES PER GALLON: _____ AVERAGE COST OF FUEL PER GALLON: _____

MAINTENANCE RECORD

DATE	REPAIR FACILITY	REPAIRS DESCRIPTION	PO#	COST

NOTES:

DRIVER LOG BOOK

DRIVERS NAME: _____   COMPANY: _____   WEEK: _____

TRUCK NUMBER	STARTING ODOMETER READING	ENDING ODOMETER READING	TOTAL DISTANCE

TRIP RECORD

DATE	TRAILER	ORIGIN CITY	DESTINATION CITY	MILES	RATE

TOTAL TRIPS: _____   TOTAL MILES: _____   TOTAL REVENUE: _____

FUEL PURCHASE RECORD

DATE	ODOMETER	MILES DRIVEN	GALLONS	MPG	RATE PER GALLON	TOTAL COST	NOTES

AVERAGE MILES PER GALLON: _____   AVERAGE COST OF FUEL PER GALLON: _____

MAINTENANCE RECORD

DATE	REPAIR FACILITY	REPAIRS DESCRIPTION	PO#	COST

NOTES:

_____

_____

_____

_____

DRIVER LOG BOOK

DRIVERS NAME: _____ COMPANY: _____ WEEK: _____

TRUCK NUMBER	STARTING ODOMETER READING	ENDING ODOMETER READING	TOTAL DISTANCE

TRIP RECORD

DATE	TRAILER	ORIGIN CITY	DESTINATION CITY	MILES	RATE

TOTAL TRIPS: _____ TOTAL MILES: _____ TOTAL REVENUE: _____

FUEL PURCHASE RECORD

DATE	ODOMETER	MILES DRIVEN	GALLONS	MPG	RATE PER GALLON	TOTAL COST	NOTES

AVERAGE MILES PER GALLON: _____ AVERAGE COST OF FUEL PER GALLON: _____

MAINTENANCE RECORD

DATE	REPAIR FACILITY	REPAIRS DESCRIPTION	PO#	COST

NOTES:

DRIVER LOG BOOK

DRIVERS NAME: _____   COMPANY: _____   WEEK: _____

TRUCK NUMBER	STARTING ODOMETER READING	ENDING ODOMETER READING	TOTAL DISTANCE

TRIP RECORD

DATE	TRAILER	ORIGIN CITY	DESTINATION CITY	MILES	RATE

TOTAL TRIPS: _____   TOTAL MILES: _____   TOTAL REVENUE: _____

FUEL PURCHASE RECORD

DATE	ODOMETER	MILES DRIVEN	GALLONS	MPG	RATE PER GALLON	TOTAL COST	NOTES

AVERAGE MILES PER GALLON: _____   AVERAGE COST OF FUEL PER GALLON: _____

MAINTENANCE RECORD

DATE	REPAIR FACILITY	REPAIRS DESCRIPTION	PO#	COST

NOTES:
_____
_____
_____

Driver Log Book

DRIVERS NAME: _____ COMPANY: _____ WEEK: _____

TRUCK NUMBER	STARTING ODOMETER READING	ENDING ODOMETER READING	TOTAL DISTANCE

Trip Record

DATE	TRAILER	ORIGIN CITY	DESTINATION CITY	MILES	RATE

TOTAL TRIPS: _____ TOTAL MILES: _____ TOTAL REVENUE: _____

Fuel Purchase Record

DATE	ODOMETER	MILES DRIVEN	GALLONS	MPG	RATE PER GALLON	TOTAL COST	NOTES

AVERAGE MILES PER GALLON: _____ AVERAGE COST OF FUEL PER GALLON: _____

Maintenance Record

DATE	REPAIR FACILITY	REPAIRS DESCRIPTION	PO#	COST

NOTES:

Driver Log Book

DRIVERS NAME: _____   COMPANY: _____   WEEK: _____

TRUCK NUMBER	STARTING ODOMETER READING	ENDING ODOMETER READING	TOTAL DISTANCE

Trip Record

DATE	TRAILER	ORIGIN CITY	DESTINATION CITY	MILES	RATE

TOTAL TRIPS: _____   TOTAL MILES: _____   TOTAL REVENUE: _____

Fuel Purchase Record

DATE	ODOMETER	MILES DRIVEN	GALLONS	MPG	RATE PER GALLON	TOTAL COST	NOTES

AVERAGE MILES PER GALLON: _____   AVERAGE COST OF FUEL PER GALLON: _____

Maintenance Record

DATE	REPAIR FACILITY	REPAIRS DESCRIPTION	PO#	COST

NOTES:

_____

_____

_____

_____

DRIVER LOG BOOK

DRIVERS NAME: _____   COMPANY: _____   WEEK: _____

TRUCK NUMBER	STARTING ODOMETER READING	ENDING ODOMETER READING	TOTAL DISTANCE

TRIP RECORD

DATE	TRAILER	ORIGIN CITY	DESTINATION CITY	MILES	RATE

TOTAL TRIPS: _____   TOTAL MILES: _____   TOTAL REVENUE: _____

FUEL PURCHASE RECORD

DATE	ODOMETER	MILES DRIVEN	GALLONS	MPG	RATE PER GALLON	TOTAL COST	NOTES

AVERAGE MILES PER GALLON: _____   AVERAGE COST OF FUEL PER GALLON: _____

MAINTENANCE RECORD

DATE	REPAIR FACILITY	REPAIRS DESCRIPTION	PO#	COST

NOTES:

DRIVER LOG BOOK

DRIVERS NAME: _____ COMPANY: _____ WEEK: _____

TRUCK NUMBER	STARTING ODOMETER READING	ENDING ODOMETER READING	TOTAL DISTANCE

TRIP RECORD

DATE	TRAILER	ORIGIN CITY	DESTINATION CITY	MILES	RATE

TOTAL TRIPS: _____ TOTAL MILES: _____ TOTAL REVENUE: _____

FUEL PURCHASE RECORD

DATE	ODOMETER	MILES DRIVEN	GALLONS	MPG	RATE PER GALLON	TOTAL COST	NOTES

AVERAGE MILES PER GALLON: _____ AVERAGE COST OF FUEL PER GALLON: _____

MAINTENANCE RECORD

DATE	REPAIR FACILITY	REPAIRS DESCRIPTION	PO#	COST

NOTES:

_____

_____

_____

_____

Driver Log Book

DRIVERS NAME: _____   COMPANY: _____   WEEK: _____

TRUCK NUMBER	STARTING ODOMETER READING	ENDING ODOMETER READING	TOTAL DISTANCE

TRIP RECORD

DATE	TRAILER	ORIGIN CITY	DESTINATION CITY	MILES	RATE

TOTAL TRIPS: _____   TOTAL MILES: _____   TOTAL REVENUE: _____

FUEL PURCHASE RECORD

DATE	ODOMETER	MILES DRIVEN	GALLONS	MPG	RATE PER GALLON	TOTAL COST	NOTES

AVERAGE MILES PER GALLON: _____   AVERAGE COST OF FUEL PER GALLON: _____

MAINTENANCE RECORD

DATE	REPAIR FACILITY	REPAIRS DESCRIPTION	PO#	COST

NOTES:

Driver Log Book

DRIVERS NAME: _____   COMPANY: _____   WEEK: _____

TRUCK NUMBER	STARTING ODOMETER READING	ENDING ODOMETER READING	TOTAL DISTANCE

Trip Record

DATE	TRAILER	ORIGIN CITY	DESTINATION CITY	MILES	RATE

TOTAL TRIPS: _____   TOTAL MILES: _____   TOTAL REVENUE: _____

Fuel Purchase Record

DATE	ODOMETER	MILES DRIVEN	GALLONS	MPG	RATE PER GALLON	TOTAL COST	NOTES

AVERAGE MILES PER GALLON: _____   AVERAGE COST OF FUEL PER GALLON: _____

Maintenance Record

DATE	REPAIR FACILITY	REPAIRS DESCRIPTION	PO#	COST

NOTES:

_____

_____

_____

Driver Log Book

DRIVERS NAME: _____   COMPANY: _____   WEEK: _____

TRUCK NUMBER	STARTING ODOMETER READING	ENDING ODOMETER READING	TOTAL DISTANCE

Trip Record

DATE	TRAILER	ORIGIN CITY	DESTINATION CITY	MILES	RATE

TOTAL TRIPS:_____   TOTAL MILES:_____   TOTAL REVENUE:_____

Fuel Purchase Record

DATE	ODOMETER	MILES DRIVEN	GALLONS	MPG	RATE PER GALLON	TOTAL COST	NOTES

AVERAGE MILES PER GALLON: _____   AVERAGE COST OF FUEL PER GALLON: _____

Maintenance Record

DATE	REPAIR FACILITY	REPAIRS DESCRIPTION	PO#	COST

NOTES:

DRIVER LOG BOOK

DRIVERS NAME: _____ COMPANY: _____ WEEK: _____

TRUCK NUMBER	STARTING ODOMETER READING	ENDING ODOMETER READING	TOTAL DISTANCE

TRIP RECORD

DATE	TRAILER	ORIGIN CITY	DESTINATION CITY	MILES	RATE

TOTAL TRIPS: _____ TOTAL MILES: _____ TOTAL REVENUE: _____

FUEL PURCHASE RECORD

DATE	ODOMETER	MILES DRIVEN	GALLONS	MPG	RATE PER GALLON	TOTAL COST	NOTES

AVERAGE MILES PER GALLON: _____ AVERAGE COST OF FUEL PER GALLON: _____

MAINTENANCE RECORD

DATE	REPAIR FACILITY	REPAIRS DESCRIPTION	PO#	COST

NOTES:

_____

_____

_____

_____

Driver Log Book

DRIVERS NAME: _____   COMPANY: _____   WEEK: _____

TRUCK NUMBER	STARTING ODOMETER READING	ENDING ODOMETER READING	TOTAL DISTANCE

Trip Record

DATE	TRAILER	ORIGIN CITY	DESTINATION CITY	MILES	RATE

TOTAL TRIPS: _____   TOTAL MILES: _____   TOTAL REVENUE: _____

Fuel Purchase Record

DATE	ODOMETER	MILES DRIVEN	GALLONS	MPG	RATE PER GALLON	TOTAL COST	NOTES

AVERAGE MILES PER GALLON: _____   AVERAGE COST OF FUEL PER GALLON: _____

Maintenance Record

DATE	REPAIR FACILITY	REPAIRS DESCRIPTION	PO#	COST

NOTES:

Driver Log Book

DRIVERS NAME: _____   COMPANY: _____   WEEK: _____

TRUCK NUMBER	STARTING ODOMETER READING	ENDING ODOMETER READING	TOTAL DISTANCE

TRIP RECORD

DATE	TRAILER	ORIGIN CITY	DESTINATION CITY	MILES	RATE

TOTAL TRIPS: _____   TOTAL MILES: _____   TOTAL REVENUE: _____

FUEL PURCHASE RECORD

DATE	ODOMETER	MILES DRIVEN	GALLONS	MPG	RATE PER GALLON	TOTAL COST	NOTES

AVERAGE MILES PER GALLON: _____   AVERAGE COST OF FUEL PER GALLON: _____

MAINTENANCE RECORD

DATE	REPAIR FACILITY	REPAIRS DESCRIPTION	PO#	COST

NOTES:

_____

_____

_____

DRIVER LOG BOOK

DRIVERS NAME: _____ COMPANY: _____ WEEK: _____

TRUCK NUMBER	STARTING ODOMETER READING	ENDING ODOMETER READING	TOTAL DISTANCE

TRIP RECORD

DATE	TRAILER	ORIGIN CITY	DESTINATION CITY	MILES	RATE

TOTAL TRIPS: _____ TOTAL MILES: _____ TOTAL REVENUE: _____

FUEL PURCHASE RECORD

DATE	ODOMETER	MILES DRIVEN	GALLONS	MPG	RATE PER GALLON	TOTAL COST	NOTES

AVERAGE MILES PER GALLON: _____ AVERAGE COST OF FUEL PER GALLON: _____

MAINTENANCE RECORD

DATE	REPAIR FACILITY	REPAIRS DESCRIPTION	PO#	COST

NOTES:

Driver Log Book

DRIVERS NAME: _____ COMPANY: _____ WEEK: _____

TRUCK NUMBER	STARTING ODOMETER READING	ENDING ODOMETER READING	TOTAL DISTANCE

TRIP RECORD

DATE	TRAILER	ORIGIN CITY	DESTINATION CITY	MILES	RATE

TOTAL TRIPS: _____ TOTAL MILES: _____ TOTAL REVENUE: _____

FUEL PURCHASE RECORD

DATE	ODOMETER	MILES DRIVEN	GALLONS	MPG	RATE PER GALLON	TOTAL COST	NOTES

AVERAGE MILES PER GALLON: _____ AVERAGE COST OF FUEL PER GALLON: _____

MAINTENANCE RECORD

DATE	REPAIR FACILITY	REPAIRS DESCRIPTION	PO#	COST

NOTES:

_____

_____

_____

_____

DRIVER LOG BOOK

DRIVERS NAME: _____ COMPANY: _____ WEEK: _____

TRUCK NUMBER	STARTING ODOMETER READING	ENDING ODOMETER READING	TOTAL DISTANCE

TRIP RECORD

DATE	TRAILER	ORIGIN CITY	DESTINATION CITY	MILES	RATE

TOTAL TRIPS:_____ TOTAL MILES:_____ TOTAL REVENUE:_____

FUEL PURCHASE RECORD

DATE	ODOMETER	MILES DRIVEN	GALLONS	MPG	RATE PER GALLON	TOTAL COST	NOTES

AVERAGE MILES PER GALLON:_____ AVERAGE COST OF FUEL PER GALLON:_____

MAINTENANCE RECORD

DATE	REPAIR FACILITY	REPAIRS DESCRIPTION	PO#	COST

NOTES:

Driver Log Book

DRIVERS NAME: _____   COMPANY: _____   WEEK: _____

TRUCK NUMBER	STARTING ODOMETER READING	ENDING ODOMETER READING	TOTAL DISTANCE

TRIP RECORD

DATE	TRAILER	ORIGIN CITY	DESTINATION CITY	MILES	RATE

TOTAL TRIPS: _____   TOTAL MILES: _____   TOTAL REVENUE: _____

FUEL PURCHASE RECORD

DATE	ODOMETER	MILES DRIVEN	GALLONS	MPG	RATE PER GALLON	TOTAL COST	NOTES

AVERAGE MILES PER GALLON: _____   AVERAGE COST OF FUEL PER GALLON: _____

MAINTENANCE RECORD

DATE	REPAIR FACILITY	REPAIRS DESCRIPTION	PO#	COST

NOTES:

_____

_____

_____

_____

Driver Log Book

DRIVERS NAME: _____   COMPANY: _____   WEEK: _____

TRUCK NUMBER	STARTING ODOMETER READING	ENDING ODOMETER READING	TOTAL DISTANCE

Trip Record

DATE	TRAILER	ORIGIN CITY	DESTINATION CITY	MILES	RATE

TOTAL TRIPS: _____   TOTAL MILES: _____   TOTAL REVENUE: _____

Fuel Purchase Record

DATE	ODOMETER	MILES DRIVEN	GALLONS	MPG	RATE PER GALLON	TOTAL COST	NOTES

AVERAGE MILES PER GALLON: _____   AVERAGE COST OF FUEL PER GALLON: _____

Maintenance Record

DATE	REPAIR FACILITY	REPAIRS DESCRIPTION	PO#	COST

NOTES:

Driver Log Book

DRIVERS NAME: _____	COMPANY: _____	WEEK: _____

TRUCK NUMBER	STARTING ODOMETER READING	ENDING ODOMETER READING	TOTAL DISTANCE

TRIP RECORD

DATE	TRAILER	ORIGIN CITY	DESTINATION CITY	MILES	RATE

TOTAL TRIPS: _____   TOTAL MILES: _____   TOTAL REVENUE: _____

FUEL PURCHASE RECORD

DATE	ODOMETER	MILES DRIVEN	GALLONS	MPG	RATE PER GALLON	TOTAL COST	NOTES

AVERAGE MILES PER GALLON: _____   AVERAGE COST OF FUEL PER GALLON: _____

MAINTENANCE RECORD

DATE	REPAIR FACILITY	REPAIRS DESCRIPTION	PO#	COST

NOTES:

_____

_____

_____

_____

Driver Log Book

Drivers Name: _____ Company: _____ Week: _____

Truck Number	Starting Odometer Reading	Ending Odometer Reading	Total Distance

Trip Record

Date	Trailer	Origin City	Destination City	Miles	Rate

Total Trips: _____ Total Miles: _____ Total Revenue: _____

Fuel Purchase Record

Date	Odometer	Miles Driven	Gallons	MPG	Rate Per Gallon	Total Cost	Notes

Average Miles Per Gallon: _____ Average Cost of Fuel Per Gallon: _____

Maintenance Record

Date	Repair Facility	Repairs Description	PO#	Cost

Notes:

DRIVER LOG BOOK

DRIVERS NAME: _____   COMPANY: _____   WEEK: _____

TRUCK NUMBER	STARTING ODOMETER READING	ENDING ODOMETER READING	TOTAL DISTANCE

TRIP RECORD

DATE	TRAILER	ORIGIN CITY	DESTINATION CITY	MILES	RATE

TOTAL TRIPS: _____   TOTAL MILES: _____   TOTAL REVENUE: _____

FUEL PURCHASE RECORD

DATE	ODOMETER	MILES DRIVEN	GALLONS	MPG	RATE PER GALLON	TOTAL COST	NOTES

AVERAGE MILES PER GALLON: _____   AVERAGE COST OF FUEL PER GALLON: _____

MAINTENANCE RECORD

DATE	REPAIR FACILITY	REPAIRS DESCRIPTION	PO#	COST

NOTES:

_____

_____

_____

Driver Log Book

DRIVERS NAME: _____ COMPANY: _____ WEEK: _____

TRUCK NUMBER	STARTING ODOMETER READING	ENDING ODOMETER READING	TOTAL DISTANCE

Trip Record

DATE	TRAILER	ORIGIN CITY	DESTINATION CITY	MILES	RATE

TOTAL TRIPS: _____ TOTAL MILES: _____ TOTAL REVENUE: _____

Fuel Purchase Record

DATE	ODOMETER	MILES DRIVEN	GALLONS	MPG	RATE PER GALLON	TOTAL COST	NOTES

AVERAGE MILES PER GALLON: _____ AVERAGE COST OF FUEL PER GALLON: _____

Maintenance Record

DATE	REPAIR FACILITY	REPAIRS DESCRIPTION	PO#	COST

NOTES:

Driver Log Book

DRIVERS NAME: _____   COMPANY: _____   WEEK: _____

TRUCK NUMBER	STARTING ODOMETER READING	ENDING ODOMETER READING	TOTAL DISTANCE

TRIP RECORD

DATE	TRAILER	ORIGIN CITY	DESTINATION CITY	MILES	RATE

TOTAL TRIPS: _____   TOTAL MILES: _____   TOTAL REVENUE: _____

FUEL PURCHASE RECORD

DATE	ODOMETER	MILES DRIVEN	GALLONS	MPG	RATE PER GALLON	TOTAL COST	NOTES

AVERAGE MILES PER GALLON: _____   AVERAGE COST OF FUEL PER GALLON: _____

MAINTENANCE RECORD

DATE	REPAIR FACILITY	REPAIRS DESCRIPTION	PO#	COST

NOTES:

_____
_____
_____

DRIVER LOG BOOK

DRIVERS NAME: _____   COMPANY: _____   WEEK: _____

TRUCK NUMBER	STARTING ODOMETER READING	ENDING ODOMETER READING	TOTAL DISTANCE

TRIP RECORD

DATE	TRAILER	ORIGIN CITY	DESTINATION CITY	MILES	RATE

TOTAL TRIPS: _____   TOTAL MILES: _____   TOTAL REVENUE: _____

FUEL PURCHASE RECORD

DATE	ODOMETER	MILES DRIVEN	GALLONS	MPG	RATE PER GALLON	TOTAL COST	NOTES

AVERAGE MILES PER GALLON: _____   AVERAGE COST OF FUEL PER GALLON: _____

MAINTENANCE RECORD

DATE	REPAIR FACILITY	REPAIRS DESCRIPTION	PO#	COST

NOTES:

DRIVER LOG BOOK

DRIVERS NAME: _____ COMPANY: _____ WEEK: _____

TRUCK NUMBER	STARTING ODOMETER READING	ENDING ODOMETER READING	TOTAL DISTANCE

TRIP RECORD

DATE	TRAILER	ORIGIN CITY	DESTINATION CITY	MILES	RATE

TOTAL TRIPS: _____ TOTAL MILES: _____ TOTAL REVENUE: _____

FUEL PURCHASE RECORD

DATE	ODOMETER	MILES DRIVEN	GALLONS	MPG	RATE PER GALLON	TOTAL COST	NOTES

AVERAGE MILES PER GALLON: _____ AVERAGE COST OF FUEL PER GALLON: _____

MAINTENANCE RECORD

DATE	REPAIR FACILITY	REPAIRS DESCRIPTION	PO#	COST

NOTES:

_____

_____

_____

DRIVER LOG BOOK

DRIVERS NAME: _____ COMPANY: _____ WEEK: _____

TRUCK NUMBER	STARTING ODOMETER READING	ENDING ODOMETER READING	TOTAL DISTANCE

TRIP RECORD

DATE	TRAILER	ORIGIN CITY	DESTINATION CITY	MILES	RATE

TOTAL TRIPS:_____ TOTAL MILES:_____ TOTAL REVENUE:_____

FUEL PURCHASE RECORD

DATE	ODOMETER	MILES DRIVEN	GALLONS	MPG	RATE PER GALLON	TOTAL COST	NOTES

AVERAGE MILES PER GALLON:_____ AVERAGE COST OF FUEL PER GALLON:_____

MAINTENANCE RECORD

DATE	REPAIR FACILITY	REPAIRS DESCRIPTION	PO#	COST

NOTES:

Driver Log Book

DRIVERS NAME: _____ COMPANY: _____ WEEK: _____

TRUCK NUMBER	STARTING ODOMETER READING	ENDING ODOMETER READING	TOTAL DISTANCE

TRIP RECORD

DATE	TRAILER	ORIGIN CITY	DESTINATION CITY	MILES	RATE

TOTAL TRIPS: _____ TOTAL MILES: _____ TOTAL REVENUE: _____

FUEL PURCHASE RECORD

DATE	ODOMETER	MILES DRIVEN	GALLONS	MPG	RATE PER GALLON	TOTAL COST	NOTES

AVERAGE MILES PER GALLON: _____ AVERAGE COST OF FUEL PER GALLON: _____

MAINTENANCE RECORD

DATE	REPAIR FACILITY	REPAIRS DESCRIPTION	PO#	COST

NOTES:

_____

_____

_____

_____

DRIVER LOG BOOK

DRIVERS NAME: _____ COMPANY: _____ WEEK: _____

TRUCK NUMBER	STARTING ODOMETER READING	ENDING ODOMETER READING	TOTAL DISTANCE

TRIP RECORD

DATE	TRAILER	ORIGIN CITY	DESTINATION CITY	MILES	RATE

TOTAL TRIPS: _____ TOTAL MILES: _____ TOTAL REVENUE: _____

FUEL PURCHASE RECORD

DATE	ODOMETER	MILES DRIVEN	GALLONS	MPG	RATE PER GALLON	TOTAL COST	NOTES

AVERAGE MILES PER GALLON: _____ AVERAGE COST OF FUEL PER GALLON: _____

MAINTENANCE RECORD

DATE	REPAIR FACILITY	REPAIRS DESCRIPTION	PO#	COST

NOTES:

DRIVER LOG BOOK

DRIVERS NAME: _____ COMPANY: _____ WEEK: _____

TRUCK NUMBER	STARTING ODOMETER READING	ENDING ODOMETER READING	TOTAL DISTANCE

TRIP RECORD

DATE	TRAILER	ORIGIN CITY	DESTINATION CITY	MILES	RATE

TOTAL TRIPS: _____ TOTAL MILES: _____ TOTAL REVENUE: _____

FUEL PURCHASE RECORD

DATE	ODOMETER	MILES DRIVEN	GALLONS	MPG	RATE PER GALLON	TOTAL COST	NOTES

AVERAGE MILES PER GALLON: _____ AVERAGE COST OF FUEL PER GALLON: _____

MAINTENANCE RECORD

DATE	REPAIR FACILITY	REPAIRS DESCRIPTION	PO#	COST

NOTES:
_____
_____
_____

Driver Log Book

DRIVERS NAME: _____ COMPANY: _____ WEEK: _____

TRUCK NUMBER	STARTING ODOMETER READING	ENDING ODOMETER READING	TOTAL DISTANCE

TRIP RECORD

DATE	TRAILER	ORIGIN CITY	DESTINATION CITY	MILES	RATE

TOTAL TRIPS: _____ TOTAL MILES: _____ TOTAL REVENUE: _____

FUEL PURCHASE RECORD

DATE	ODOMETER	MILES DRIVEN	GALLONS	MPG	RATE PER GALLON	TOTAL COST	NOTES

AVERAGE MILES PER GALLON: _____ AVERAGE COST OF FUEL PER GALLON: _____

MAINTENANCE RECORD

DATE	REPAIR FACILITY	REPAIRS DESCRIPTION	PO#	COST

NOTES:

Driver Log Book

DRIVERS NAME: _____ COMPANY: _____ WEEK: _____

TRUCK NUMBER	STARTING ODOMETER READING	ENDING ODOMETER READING	TOTAL DISTANCE

Trip Record

DATE	TRAILER	ORIGIN CITY	DESTINATION CITY	MILES	RATE

TOTAL TRIPS: _____ TOTAL MILES: _____ TOTAL REVENUE: _____

Fuel Purchase Record

DATE	ODOMETER	MILES DRIVEN	GALLONS	MPG	RATE PER GALLON	TOTAL COST	NOTES

AVERAGE MILES PER GALLON: _____ AVERAGE COST OF FUEL PER GALLON: _____

Maintenance Record

DATE	REPAIR FACILITY	REPAIRS DESCRIPTION	PO#	COST

NOTES:

_____

_____

_____

DRIVER LOG BOOK

DRIVERS NAME: _____   COMPANY: _____   WEEK: _____

TRUCK NUMBER	STARTING ODOMETER READING	ENDING ODOMETER READING	TOTAL DISTANCE

TRIP RECORD

DATE	TRAILER	ORIGIN CITY	DESTINATION CITY	MILES	RATE

TOTAL TRIPS: _____   TOTAL MILES: _____   TOTAL REVENUE: _____

FUEL PURCHASE RECORD

DATE	ODOMETER	MILES DRIVEN	GALLONS	MPG	RATE PER GALLON	TOTAL COST	NOTES

AVERAGE MILES PER GALLON: _____   AVERAGE COST OF FUEL PER GALLON: _____

MAINTENANCE RECORD

DATE	REPAIR FACILITY	REPAIRS DESCRIPTION	PO#	COST

NOTES:

DRIVER LOG BOOK

DRIVERS NAME: _____ COMPANY: _____ WEEK: _____

TRUCK NUMBER	STARTING ODOMETER READING	ENDING ODOMETER READING	TOTAL DISTANCE

TRIP RECORD

DATE	TRAILER	ORIGIN CITY	DESTINATION CITY	MILES	RATE

TOTAL TRIPS:_____ TOTAL MILES:_____ TOTAL REVENUE:_____

FUEL PURCHASE RECORD

DATE	ODOMETER	MILES DRIVEN	GALLONS	MPG	RATE PER GALLON	TOTAL COST	NOTES

AVERAGE MILES PER GALLON: _____ AVERAGE COST OF FUEL PER GALLON: _____

MAINTENANCE RECORD

DATE	REPAIR FACILITY	REPAIRS DESCRIPTION	PO#	COST

NOTES:
_____
_____
_____

DRIVER LOG BOOK

DRIVERS NAME: _____ COMPANY: _____ WEEK: _____

TRUCK NUMBER	STARTING ODOMETER READING	ENDING ODOMETER READING	TOTAL DISTANCE

TRIP RECORD

DATE	TRAILER	ORIGIN CITY	DESTINATION CITY	MILES	RATE

TOTAL TRIPS:_____ TOTAL MILES:_____ TOTAL REVENUE:_____

FUEL PURCHASE RECORD

DATE	ODOMETER	MILES DRIVEN	GALLONS	MPG	RATE PER GALLON	TOTAL COST	NOTES

AVERAGE MILES PER GALLON: _____ AVERAGE COST OF FUEL PER GALLON: _____

MAINTENANCE RECORD

DATE	REPAIR FACILITY	REPAIRS DESCRIPTION	PO#	COST

NOTES:

Driver Log Book

DRIVERS NAME: _____ COMPANY: _____ WEEK: _____

TRUCK NUMBER	STARTING ODOMETER READING	ENDING ODOMETER READING	TOTAL DISTANCE

TRIP RECORD

DATE	TRAILER	ORIGIN CITY	DESTINATION CITY	MILES	RATE

TOTAL TRIPS: _____ TOTAL MILES: _____ TOTAL REVENUE: _____

FUEL PURCHASE RECORD

DATE	ODOMETER	MILES DRIVEN	GALLONS	MPG	RATE PER GALLON	TOTAL COST	NOTES

AVERAGE MILES PER GALLON: _____ AVERAGE COST OF FUEL PER GALLON: _____

MAINTENANCE RECORD

DATE	REPAIR FACILITY	REPAIRS DESCRIPTION	PO#	COST

NOTES:

_____

_____

_____

_____

Driver Log Book

DRIVERS NAME: _____ COMPANY: _____ WEEK: _____

TRUCK NUMBER	STARTING ODOMETER READING	ENDING ODOMETER READING	TOTAL DISTANCE

Trip Record

DATE	TRAILER	ORIGIN CITY	DESTINATION CITY	MILES	RATE

TOTAL TRIPS: _____ TOTAL MILES: _____ TOTAL REVENUE: _____

Fuel Purchase Record

DATE	ODOMETER	MILES DRIVEN	GALLONS	MPG	RATE PER GALLON	TOTAL COST	NOTES

AVERAGE MILES PER GALLON: _____ AVERAGE COST OF FUEL PER GALLON: _____

Maintenance Record

DATE	REPAIR FACILITY	REPAIRS DESCRIPTION	PO#	COST

NOTES:

DRIVER LOG BOOK

DRIVERS NAME: _____   COMPANY: _____   WEEK: _____

TRUCK NUMBER	STARTING ODOMETER READING	ENDING ODOMETER READING	TOTAL DISTANCE

TRIP RECORD

DATE	TRAILER	ORIGIN CITY	DESTINATION CITY	MILES	RATE

TOTAL TRIPS: _____   TOTAL MILES: _____   TOTAL REVENUE: _____

FUEL PURCHASE RECORD

DATE	ODOMETER	MILES DRIVEN	GALLONS	MPG	RATE PER GALLON	TOTAL COST	NOTES

AVERAGE MILES PER GALLON: _____   AVERAGE COST OF FUEL PER GALLON: _____

MAINTENANCE RECORD

DATE	REPAIR FACILITY	REPAIRS DESCRIPTION	PO#	COST

NOTES:

_____

_____

_____

Driver Log Book

DRIVERS NAME: _____ COMPANY: _____ WEEK: _____

TRUCK NUMBER	STARTING ODOMETER READING	ENDING ODOMETER READING	TOTAL DISTANCE

TRIP RECORD

DATE	TRAILER	ORIGIN CITY	DESTINATION CITY	MILES	RATE

TOTAL TRIPS: _____ TOTAL MILES: _____ TOTAL REVENUE: _____

FUEL PURCHASE RECORD

DATE	ODOMETER	MILES DRIVEN	GALLONS	MPG	RATE PER GALLON	TOTAL COST	NOTES

AVERAGE MILES PER GALLON: _____ AVERAGE COST OF FUEL PER GALLON: _____

MAINTENANCE RECORD

DATE	REPAIR FACILITY	REPAIRS DESCRIPTION	PO#	COST

NOTES:

Driver Log Book

DRIVERS NAME: _____   COMPANY: _____   WEEK: _____

TRUCK NUMBER	STARTING ODOMETER READING	ENDING ODOMETER READING	TOTAL DISTANCE

TRIP RECORD

DATE	TRAILER	ORIGIN CITY	DESTINATION CITY	MILES	RATE

TOTAL TRIPS: _____   TOTAL MILES: _____   TOTAL REVENUE: _____

FUEL PURCHASE RECORD

DATE	ODOMETER	MILES DRIVEN	GALLONS	MPG	RATE PER GALLON	TOTAL COST	NOTES

AVERAGE MILES PER GALLON: _____   AVERAGE COST OF FUEL PER GALLON: _____

MAINTENANCE RECORD

DATE	REPAIR FACILITY	REPAIRS DESCRIPTION	PO#	COST

NOTES:

_____

_____

_____

DRIVER LOG BOOK

DRIVERS NAME: _____ COMPANY: _____ WEEK: _____

TRUCK NUMBER	STARTING ODOMETER READING	ENDING ODOMETER READING	TOTAL DISTANCE

TRIP RECORD

DATE	TRAILER	ORIGIN CITY	DESTINATION CITY	MILES	RATE

TOTAL TRIPS: _____ TOTAL MILES: _____ TOTAL REVENUE: _____

FUEL PURCHASE RECORD

DATE	ODOMETER	MILES DRIVEN	GALLONS	MPG	RATE PER GALLON	TOTAL COST	NOTES

AVERAGE MILES PER GALLON: _____ AVERAGE COST OF FUEL PER GALLON: _____

MAINTENANCE RECORD

DATE	REPAIR FACILITY	REPAIRS DESCRIPTION	PO#	COST

NOTES:

DRIVER LOG BOOK

DRIVERS NAME: _____ COMPANY: _____ WEEK: _____

TRUCK NUMBER	STARTING ODOMETER READING	ENDING ODOMETER READING	TOTAL DISTANCE

TRIP RECORD

DATE	TRAILER	ORIGIN CITY	DESTINATION CITY	MILES	RATE

TOTAL TRIPS: _____ TOTAL MILES: _____ TOTAL REVENUE: _____

FUEL PURCHASE RECORD

DATE	ODOMETER	MILES DRIVEN	GALLONS	MPG	RATE PER GALLON	TOTAL COST	NOTES

AVERAGE MILES PER GALLON: _____ AVERAGE COST OF FUEL PER GALLON: _____

MAINTENANCE RECORD

DATE	REPAIR FACILITY	REPAIRS DESCRIPTION	PO#	COST

NOTES:

_____

_____

_____

_____

Driver Log Book

DRIVERS NAME: _____   COMPANY: _____   WEEK: _____

TRUCK NUMBER	STARTING ODOMETER READING	ENDING ODOMETER READING	TOTAL DISTANCE

Trip Record

DATE	TRAILER	ORIGIN CITY	DESTINATION CITY	MILES	RATE

TOTAL TRIPS: _____   TOTAL MILES: _____   TOTAL REVENUE: _____

Fuel Purchase Record

DATE	ODOMETER	MILES DRIVEN	GALLONS	MPG	RATE PER GALLON	TOTAL COST	NOTES

AVERAGE MILES PER GALLON: _____   AVERAGE COST OF FUEL PER GALLON: _____

Maintenance Record

DATE	REPAIR FACILITY	REPAIRS DESCRIPTION	PO#	COST

NOTES:

DRIVER LOG BOOK

DRIVERS NAME: _____   COMPANY: _____   WEEK: _____

TRUCK NUMBER	STARTING ODOMETER READING	ENDING ODOMETER READING	TOTAL DISTANCE

TRIP RECORD

DATE	TRAILER	ORIGIN CITY	DESTINATION CITY	MILES	RATE

TOTAL TRIPS: _____   TOTAL MILES: _____   TOTAL REVENUE: _____

FUEL PURCHASE RECORD

DATE	ODOMETER	MILES DRIVEN	GALLONS	MPG	RATE PER GALLON	TOTAL COST	NOTES

AVERAGE MILES PER GALLON: _____   AVERAGE COST OF FUEL PER GALLON: _____

MAINTENANCE RECORD

DATE	REPAIR FACILITY	REPAIRS DESCRIPTION	PO#	COST

NOTES: _____
_____
_____
_____

Driver Log Book

DRIVERS NAME: _____   COMPANY: _____   WEEK: _____

TRUCK NUMBER	STARTING ODOMETER READING	ENDING ODOMETER READING	TOTAL DISTANCE

TRIP RECORD

DATE	TRAILER	ORIGIN CITY	DESTINATION CITY	MILES	RATE

TOTAL TRIPS: _____   TOTAL MILES: _____   TOTAL REVENUE: _____

FUEL PURCHASE RECORD

DATE	ODOMETER	MILES DRIVEN	GALLONS	MPG	RATE PER GALLON	TOTAL COST	NOTES

AVERAGE MILES PER GALLON: _____   AVERAGE COST OF FUEL PER GALLON: _____

MAINTENANCE RECORD

DATE	REPAIR FACILITY	REPAIRS DESCRIPTION	PO#	COST

NOTES:

Driver Log Book

DRIVERS NAME: _____   COMPANY: _____   WEEK: _____

TRUCK NUMBER	STARTING ODOMETER READING	ENDING ODOMETER READING	TOTAL DISTANCE

TRIP RECORD

DATE	TRAILER	ORIGIN CITY	DESTINATION CITY	MILES	RATE

TOTAL TRIPS: _____   TOTAL MILES: _____   TOTAL REVENUE: _____

FUEL PURCHASE RECORD

DATE	ODOMETER	MILES DRIVEN	GALLONS	MPG	RATE PER GALLON	TOTAL COST	NOTES

AVERAGE MILES PER GALLON: _____   AVERAGE COST OF FUEL PER GALLON: _____

MAINTENANCE RECORD

DATE	REPAIR FACILITY	REPAIRS DESCRIPTION	PO#	COST

NOTES:

_____

_____

_____

Driver Log Book

DRIVERS NAME: _____ COMPANY: _____ WEEK: _____

TRUCK NUMBER	STARTING ODOMETER READING	ENDING ODOMETER READING	TOTAL DISTANCE

Trip Record

DATE	TRAILER	ORIGIN CITY	DESTINATION CITY	MILES	RATE

TOTAL TRIPS:_____ TOTAL MILES:_____ TOTAL REVENUE:_____

Fuel Purchase Record

DATE	ODOMETER	MILES DRIVEN	GALLONS	MPG	RATE PER GALLON	TOTAL COST	NOTES

AVERAGE MILES PER GALLON:_____ AVERAGE COST OF FUEL PER GALLON:_____

Maintenance Record

DATE	REPAIR FACILITY	REPAIRS DESCRIPTION	PO#	COST

NOTES:

Driver Log Book

DRIVERS NAME: _____ COMPANY: _____ WEEK: _____

TRUCK NUMBER	STARTING ODOMETER READING	ENDING ODOMETER READING	TOTAL DISTANCE

TRIP RECORD

DATE	TRAILER	ORIGIN CITY	DESTINATION CITY	MILES	RATE

TOTAL TRIPS: _____ TOTAL MILES: _____ TOTAL REVENUE: _____

FUEL PURCHASE RECORD

DATE	ODOMETER	MILES DRIVEN	GALLONS	MPG	RATE PER GALLON	TOTAL COST	NOTES

AVERAGE MILES PER GALLON: _____ AVERAGE COST OF FUEL PER GALLON: _____

MAINTENANCE RECORD

DATE	REPAIR FACILITY	REPAIRS DESCRIPTION	PO#	COST

NOTES:

_____

_____

_____

_____

DRIVER LOG BOOK

DRIVERS NAME: _____ COMPANY: _____ WEEK: _____

TRUCK NUMBER	STARTING ODOMETER READING	ENDING ODOMETER READING	TOTAL DISTANCE

TRIP RECORD

DATE	TRAILER	ORIGIN CITY	DESTINATION CITY	MILES	RATE

TOTAL TRIPS:_____ TOTAL MILES:_____ TOTAL REVENUE:_____

FUEL PURCHASE RECORD

DATE	ODOMETER	MILES DRIVEN	GALLONS	MPG	RATE PER GALLON	TOTAL COST	NOTES

AVERAGE MILES PER GALLON: _____ AVERAGE COST OF FUEL PER GALLON: _____

MAINTENANCE RECORD

DATE	REPAIR FACILITY	REPAIRS DESCRIPTION	PO#	COST

NOTES:

DRIVER LOG BOOK

DRIVERS NAME: _____   COMPANY: _____   WEEK: _____

TRUCK NUMBER	STARTING ODOMETER READING	ENDING ODOMETER READING	TOTAL DISTANCE

TRIP RECORD

DATE	TRAILER	ORIGIN CITY	DESTINATION CITY	MILES	RATE

TOTAL TRIPS: _____   TOTAL MILES: _____   TOTAL REVENUE: _____

FUEL PURCHASE RECORD

DATE	ODOMETER	MILES DRIVEN	GALLONS	MPG	RATE PER GALLON	TOTAL COST	NOTES

AVERAGE MILES PER GALLON: _____   AVERAGE COST OF FUEL PER GALLON: _____

MAINTENANCE RECORD

DATE	REPAIR FACILITY	REPAIRS DESCRIPTION	PO#	COST

NOTES:

_____

_____

_____

_____

DRIVER LOG BOOK

DRIVERS NAME: _____   COMPANY: _____   WEEK: _____

TRUCK NUMBER	STARTING ODOMETER READING	ENDING ODOMETER READING	TOTAL DISTANCE

TRIP RECORD

DATE	TRAILER	ORIGIN CITY	DESTINATION CITY	MILES	RATE

TOTAL TRIPS:_____   TOTAL MILES:_____   TOTAL REVENUE:_____

FUEL PURCHASE RECORD

DATE	ODOMETER	MILES DRIVEN	GALLONS	MPG	RATE PER GALLON	TOTAL COST	NOTES

AVERAGE MILES PER GALLON: _____   AVERAGE COST OF FUEL PER GALLON: _____

MAINTENANCE RECORD

DATE	REPAIR FACILITY	REPAIRS DESCRIPTION	PO#	COST

NOTES:

Driver Log Book

DRIVERS NAME: _____   COMPANY: _____   WEEK: _____

TRUCK NUMBER	STARTING ODOMETER READING	ENDING ODOMETER READING	TOTAL DISTANCE

Trip Record

DATE	TRAILER	ORIGIN CITY	DESTINATION CITY	MILES	RATE

TOTAL TRIPS: _____   TOTAL MILES: _____   TOTAL REVENUE: _____

Fuel Purchase Record

DATE	ODOMETER	MILES DRIVEN	GALLONS	MPG	RATE PER GALLON	TOTAL COST	NOTES

AVERAGE MILES PER GALLON: _____   AVERAGE COST OF FUEL PER GALLON: _____

Maintenance Record

DATE	REPAIR FACILITY	REPAIRS DESCRIPTION	PO#	COST

NOTES:
_____
_____
_____
_____

DRIVER LOG BOOK

DRIVERS NAME: _____ COMPANY: _____ WEEK: _____

TRUCK NUMBER	STARTING ODOMETER READING	ENDING ODOMETER READING	TOTAL DISTANCE

TRIP RECORD

DATE	TRAILER	ORIGIN CITY	DESTINATION CITY	MILES	RATE

TOTAL TRIPS: _____ TOTAL MILES: _____ TOTAL REVENUE: _____

FUEL PURCHASE RECORD

DATE	ODOMETER	MILES DRIVEN	GALLONS	MPG	RATE PER GALLON	TOTAL COST	NOTES

AVERAGE MILES PER GALLON: _____ AVERAGE COST OF FUEL PER GALLON: _____

MAINTENANCE RECORD

DATE	REPAIR FACILITY	REPAIRS DESCRIPTION	PO#	COST

NOTES:

DRIVER LOG BOOK

DRIVERS NAME: _____ COMPANY: _____ WEEK: _____

TRUCK NUMBER	STARTING ODOMETER READING	ENDING ODOMETER READING	TOTAL DISTANCE

TRIP RECORD

DATE	TRAILER	ORIGIN CITY	DESTINATION CITY	MILES	RATE

TOTAL TRIPS:_____ TOTAL MILES:_____ TOTAL REVENUE:_____

FUEL PURCHASE RECORD

DATE	ODOMETER	MILES DRIVEN	GALLONS	MPG	RATE PER GALLON	TOTAL COST	NOTES

AVERAGE MILES PER GALLON: _____ AVERAGE COST OF FUEL PER GALLON: _____

MAINTENANCE RECORD

DATE	REPAIR FACILITY	REPAIRS DESCRIPTION	PO#	COST

NOTES:

_____

_____

_____

Driver Log Book

DRIVERS NAME: _____ COMPANY: _____ WEEK: _____

TRUCK NUMBER	STARTING ODOMETER READING	ENDING ODOMETER READING	TOTAL DISTANCE

Trip Record

DATE	TRAILER	ORIGIN CITY	DESTINATION CITY	MILES	RATE

TOTAL TRIPS: _____ TOTAL MILES: _____ TOTAL REVENUE: _____

Fuel Purchase Record

DATE	ODOMETER	MILES DRIVEN	GALLONS	MPG	RATE PER GALLON	TOTAL COST	NOTES

AVERAGE MILES PER GALLON: _____ AVERAGE COST OF FUEL PER GALLON: _____

Maintenance Record

DATE	REPAIR FACILITY	REPAIRS DESCRIPTION	PO#	COST

NOTES:

DRIVER LOG BOOK

DRIVERS NAME: _____   COMPANY: _____   WEEK: _____

TRUCK NUMBER	STARTING ODOMETER READING	ENDING ODOMETER READING	TOTAL DISTANCE

TRIP RECORD

DATE	TRAILER	ORIGIN CITY	DESTINATION CITY	MILES	RATE

TOTAL TRIPS: _____   TOTAL MILES: _____   TOTAL REVENUE: _____

FUEL PURCHASE RECORD

DATE	ODOMETER	MILES DRIVEN	GALLONS	MPG	RATE PER GALLON	TOTAL COST	NOTES

AVERAGE MILES PER GALLON: _____   AVERAGE COST OF FUEL PER GALLON: _____

MAINTENANCE RECORD

DATE	REPAIR FACILITY	REPAIRS DESCRIPTION	PO#	COST

NOTES:

_____

_____

_____

Hello

Thank you so much for purchasing our book.

Please rate the book with the stars it deserves and write your opinion, your review helps us improve our quality.

Thank you very much!

Made in the USA
Monee, IL
30 November 2021

83474516R00061